THE MINUTES
NO ONE OWNS

THE MINUTES
NO ONE OWNS

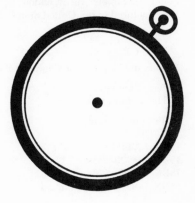

BRENDAN
GALVIN

Published by the University of Pittsburgh Press, Pittsburgh, Pa. 15260
Copyright © 1977, Brendan Galvin
All rights reserved
Feffer and Simons, Inc., London
Manufactured in the United States of America

Library of Congress Cataloging in Publication Data

Galvin, Brendan
  The minutes no one owns.

  (Pitt poetry series)
  I. Title.
PS3557.A44M5   811'.5'4   77-73464
ISBN 0-8229-3359-4
ISBN 0-8229-5286-6 pbk.
ISBN 0-8229-3364-0 lim. ed.

Acknowledgment is made to the following publications for permission to re-
print poems that appear in this book: *Ascent, The Back Door, California
Quarterly, Concerning Poetry, The Fiddlehead, Ironwood, The Little Review,
Paris Review, Poetry Northwest, Three Rivers Poetry Journal,* and *Wisconsin
Review.*

The poem "To Be Hung in a Dormitory Room" appeared originally in *College
English.* Copyright © March 1976 by the National Council of Teachers of
English. Reprinted by permission.

The poems "North-Northeast," "A Photo of Miners," "A Death in the Marsh,"
"The Old Clothes," and "Glass" appeared originally in *The New Yorker.*

Grateful acknowledgment is made to the National Endowment for the Arts for
a creative writing fellowship under which many of these poems were written
and to Central Connecticut State College for a sabbatical year during which
this collection was completed.

for
Ellen
Peter
Anne

CONTENTS

Three

NORTH-NORTHEAST

Last evening,
listening for owls,
cold filled the caves
of my chest:
fear for a second
I'd inhaled the first star.

All night this coast
was chewed and spit back
on itself, crossed
with tides, channels
adrift in their beds,
this house was
a test of wind against glass,
rainy spikes hammered home.

I kept waking to
the trickle, somewhere,
of water driven to enter
a weakness in wood,
or the too-human
cackle of something
wandering in the static
above dreams.

Wet trunks alive
with the barium glow of moss.
Red pine duff;
a heel's depth below,
sand waiting for
any mover.

This morning my shoulders
ache, sockets of freshly
wrenched wings.

3

A DEATH IN THE MARSH

1

Crammed into orange vests,
their faces burning with wind
and whiskey,
hunters were popping off
on rabbits hills away,
but the dogs were below the house,
then on the marsh
where a skinny creek
staggered out through
winter *Spartina* —
two mongrels,
a black and a gold,
yapping across opposite banks,
harrowing something,
a sleek head between them
in the water. Muskrat?
But binoculars took in
the eyestrip,
the claws raised to incisors.

2

The gold mutt yelled behind it,
hackles stiff as quills,
blocking a way;
and neck deep, the raccoon
swiping, backpedaling;
the black one bridging water
to the gold;
coon flashing into empty grass,
both of them
on the grizzled hump.
Gone.

Whanging a ladle and pan,
I made trees shiver.
Grass flailed up growls
and the whole triptych
again, coon in the creek
spitting into the jowls
of the black dog worrying it,
overleaping them.
Then the grovels of low business.

3

And the petty thief's shadow
scuffling on quilts of mulch,
its owl quaver
and funnel of cries down the dark?
Dispatched
to omnivorous heaven
to throw back the bolts
of swill sheds,
to ramble the spectrum of eats?
Between us and other deaths
always some distance.
Always this question
in the minutes no one owns.
Even the grosbeaks paused
at haggling seeds,
and the dogs,
small in a lull of wind:
occasional earflop,
spot of grass turning gold
as though from a quick
patch of sun,
whimper of licked cuts.

On all those acres
not a bleached spear out of place,
and they crawled to firmer ground,
blood seeded with wandering,
while I counted seventeen houses
on the hills.

LISTENING TO AN OLD HOUSE
IN WINTER

This house is the cold's voice box,
and the cold is making cracks about
the apple buds outside,
about what fuzzy promises they are,
and how it's going to try
each corner of this place,
wedging its snout to test
the fit of wood.
Without chewing
a single joist into excelsior,
it's going to nest in dressers
and hang the beards of
northern gods on every wall.

Already it's unstrung
pea vines, and now
it's snapping to itself because
it wants a stare like
a blue clang from ground zero,
something that will nail crows
on the yawing edge of distance
flat.

Cold says it's going to set up
in your pockets,
and squeeze the color from
your last red cent.
It doesn't like the way
it had to come here,
a moonrise at a time
and stiffening to a presence that
no chimney screen could stop.
It likes how pines keep
sweeping the moon away.

CHRISTMAS IN THE SUMMER COLONY

1

Looking with no luck for plain
silver tinsel, not blue or gold
plastic boas, or angel hair like
the tents of caterpillars,
going by the Wheelhouse I see
that my brother is in there,
wearing the overcoat
of a late literary critic
whose body was a pedestal for his head,
and the suede slippers with pilgrim buckles
that belonged to an exiled
White Russian, all bought
at the thrift shop for under two dollars.

2

My brother and I are passing ales
with the time of day. In here
you watch what you say because
the whole Pie Alley Gang
is watching what you say,
and Mr. C. A. Lieu, and the two
fishermen named after islands,
Big and Little Grease. After
the Republic Pictures sunset
the open road comes here:
the bigamous jugglers
and welfare buccaneers with dependents
christened Heather and LaDawn.
Even the last oysterman's in here
trying to patch it up with his wife
for the holidays. She sits
watching him from the bar,
proud to her shy cheekbones

that her man has kept the beast in him
alive. Like a great-gutted bird
a storm has blown ashore,
or a vast image out of *Ostrea mundi,*
though no pearl, he's dreaming
on his feet of summer nights in his
panel truck, the college girl
who said he's a real man.
A whiff of his clothes and you know
the oyster's his world.
Soon there'll be no more like him,
a New Yorker who looks like he's
melting a small animal's kidney
under his tongue will bid on their place
for back taxes and paint it cranberry.

                3
Now my brother and I
are zipping down on Shoreline Drive,
passing more ales, then stumbling for
a tree we spotted last September.
Not thinking very hard for anyone,
he mumbles about symbolic
redistribution of the wealth.
I look over my shoulder, but it's only
Orion dragging himself somewhere,
the karma of stud hopes, worn out,
thinking how bad he's going to feel
tomorrow. My brother bends the tree,
three chops and it's done,
like a turkey's neck on the block.
Coming down my path, a green load on,
I consider wrapping my love's
blue beads in oak leaves.

9

FATHER MAPPLE PREPARES
A SERMON IN HEAVEN

"Woe to him who seeks to pour oil upon the waters when God has brewed them into a gale! Woe to him who seeks to please rather than to appal! — *Moby Dick*, chapter 9.

This time he'll propound upon six men
in lumber jackets working the single,
boxed and flagged remains the sea coughed up
gingerly down St. Peter's steps,
and the widow following in slacks and scarf,
each line in her face a 4 A.M. tide.

Hope gets stoven, he'll say, spilling
the lees of thin shares and hard sites
on a dragger caught in a queer sea,
dropped below floating factories
who trawl foreign steel over anyone's gear;

though *fo'c's'le* and *Land's End* set something
in us clicking like tourist cameras,
no man can navigate five-story buoys
the drillers cut loose, though that man's
grandfather rowed in his nineties to lobsters,
and hauled his pots by hand,

though he saw winters out with Skully Joes
and back-of-the-stove kale soup,
and sometimes caroled for warmth
on a bed turned broken schooner
drifting over the banks.

Shipmates, he'll say, the grandsons turned
CPAs, or harness the water table with Stilsons
and torches in summer people's cellars,
everyone knocks off at five
to swap cigarettes with new Vikings
anchored in Buzzards Bay,

and whole school systems
lunch on fishy squares processed in Asia.
Creased men like MCs out to pasture
concoct slicks of fear and specific gravity,
spilling them over the lost *Nokomis,*
the *Cora McKay* and *Lafayette,*

until murres wash up on Monomoy,
wings pinned with number 6 fuel, feet panicking
as they shove for surf, breasts keeling sand
like animals with forelegs shot away,

and having seen another set of lights
slide out beyond the pines and drop from sight
around Wood End, leaving middle men behind,

today in a beam-cracking voice his text will be
Noah sunk in his middle years, sad girth to bet
the race on when the sea beaked and clawed
and everywhere curled a white lip and rolled
till eyeballs rolled, and how he sailed.

SLUGS

In the beginning
earth was already
collapsed, molten,
pocked with fumaroles,
older than it would be
again.

Before the moon
hummed in mud
and the stones
unhinged, cracking
like dry pods,
and the sledge heads
of tortoises for the
first time lifted,

slugs mused under leaves
in the drowning
sulfur light. They
rode down grass-blades
with the conviction of
original envy,
reamed the wild
cucumbers, leaving
husks smeared with
a glitter like thin ice,
nudged and browsed among
the continents.

Prehensile, pudendous,
gesturing with black,
retractable fingers,
one of them whispered,
biding time, at the
threshold of an ear.

THE FREEFLOATER

Midsummer: he wakes to the midnight
invitations of the marsh, or is it only
guests on a lawn somewhere, leaving a party?

In the dark he picks his way
among dreaming swaths of fog. Above him,
between branches, stars and the space
between stars,

                    then the breath-stopping
effluence of eelgrass and foot-sucking
mud, awake with the clicking tools

of night-shifting crabs, the pervasiveness
of a moon rounding over water.
He remembers his wife,

                    asleep like a fixed star
on the hill above him. Without him to man them
his sleep clothes go under, and he wades

until coolness is ringing his flanks,
then drifts off the earth on his back,
tuning to pockets of cold, tugs and sways of
direction where channels move deep.

                    Keeping to midstream
is a matter of casual sculling with cupped hands,
and sometime he sleeps, or a turtle's shield
fading its spots into depth

is as real as this long-legged
woman rising in the cerements of her hair,
a single thumbline of blood
                    on each flashing thigh.

Water whirls past like the after pools from
an oar, there is flotsam of fog, on the edge
a pussy-footed splash, then
the single *glunk* of an animal submerging.

Light on his left side.

On shore a grey blue heron,
hunching to be a stone, failing
and bowing into a curtain of reeds.

Small in his slow unwinding
under the marshaling clouds,
he thinks of a bone canoe

paddling this maze forever, and known only
to muskrats. Rounding a bend
he rolls face down

into water lit
like a midnight department store: eels
unsnag and dart down another corridor

and he steers off the bars
scrabbled with bird prints and pried shells.

There are moss-haunted logs,
mud-wall caves, the viscid backwater
                              of minnows

scattering like type from a printer's tray
when he stands to the air in his
mud rags, unsheathing his spine
to the first cold edge of fear.

RUNNING

Experts say for me to do it well
I should be forty pounds lighter
or twenty-one inches taller,

so if I do it I'm a fool,
fat fool if I don't.
Dying of experts, I shuck off

home by the back door,
taking myself to yappers at heels
and the nameless worst who may

break anywhere from bushes,
my mind holding its hand,
telling itself the teeth of the unknown

dissolve when confronted even in fear.
If you see me and toot, I may have
only my middle finger for you:

I'm not sponsored by the National
Park Service for your viewing pleasure,
have had shin splints, and suffer

permanently from Morton's Foot.
Experts say any moment my spine
may collapse from cervix to coccyx.

But look, there is heavy traffic of bees
in the burst willow catkins, that kingfisher
dips and rises over the marsh

like a lesson in scansion.
A month from here, swallows will loop and dive,
slicing the air close to my doubling heartbeat,

two months and a woodcock
will sail through a steep
parabola ending in bushes.

I let a fly live completely a moment
in the dampening bush of my hair.
Rhythms are breaking, the last shred of

human song just flew out of my head.
Once I awaited adrenalin's uppercut under
my limping heart, and paused like

a man in mid-celebration
recalled to final things. Red fish
school up in the blood. Whatever I need,

there's no name for it, but we are
a naturally healthy people,
being of the Elect, so this must be

somehow un-American. Any minute now,
Flab will dust me off with his Pontiac,
but here on the edge of energy

I believe even the stumps will fly again.
What expert ever saw a hawk go before him
toward a quarter-moon pale in the western sky,

or a random butterfly exploring the air
over bayberries? All things are pilgrims,
except maybe the blacksnake soaking up

asphalt's watery heat, who is only inertia
to be overcome. Shifts change in the blood,
but I'm breaking no records. By mile four

I'm only the framework a breeze passes through.
Bellies of gulls on the flats
are lit like quarts of milk. This wobbling

under my ribs dessicates bad habits.
I slow to a trot, to the least piper's
whistling, and my pulse begins its

shorebird glossolalia. It says
dowitcher   coot   yellowlegs
brant   bufflehead   knot

GLASS

What the warbler must have seen
was the world swung round;
without turning back
she was flying into
a distance already passed through:

another side of the woodpile
she had just cleared in a single pitch,
and beyond, through the middle ground
of pines, the background glitter
of running sea she had skipped above
like a flat stone thrown so well
it touches down on water
all the way to the other shore.

Swung round,
only slightly blurred.
Trees twinning,
far water grained,
air of a density . . .

then that split-second insight

into splashes of newspaper
and clothing,
filtered through
final dusts of light.

As perhaps,
in our last seconds,
we are swung round
to live ourselves back through
each particular,
to fall faster and faster
out of loves, out of
changes of clothes,

whole snows lifting skyward
becoming autumn leaves lifting
back into green trees,
the dead stepping out of
crumbling loam,

at the last, seed and egg
unraveling, falling away.

And all
in the time
it takes a flat stone to skip over water
and be let in.

JUMPING THE GRAVE-SIZED HOLE

There are still a few places
not sold to people in tennis whites

whose flesh is tanned like old pennies,
whose cars block traffic all August at the P.O.

It's October, aftershocks of surf rush back
into the trees, filling the absence of small talk,

and though pole beans extend themselves still,
looping along fishing line,

still forcing out a few, popcornlike blossoms,
somewhere in the earth a drain has opened,

the garden is sinking, the corn waits in its bandages
for winter. I walk up a sand road

hemmed by wild blackberries, an unseen bird
hunting and pecking the underwood's last morsels,

and it comes home stronger that
the faces of my children will mingle with other faces

and come back with only a feature or two of mine,
and someday a stranger will take his daughter

by the hand to show her these mushrooms
pushing through edges of asphalt, wearing its grains

on their lumpen hats. Farther in, jumping
the grave-sized hole a realtor dug to keep out

kids and campers, I duck under dead, rain-softened trees
crisscrossing the road: charred beer cans and kindling,

lobster husks faded pink, and on the hogsback ridge,
a steep half mile above the sporadic whine of a car,

a burnt-out house like a rotten tooth: one white wall
standing, the whole kitchen tumbled

into the cellar, enduring oxidation's
cold burn, and tall as a man this year,

the stripling poplar rooted in a mattress
flashes metallic lights as if to say no sale is final,

each purchase may be redeemed. This could be the set
some New England Wagner cooked up, but no baritone

steps out of mottled scrub to deliver an aria
from the promontory beam ending in char above the debris.

The histrionic bathtub levitates on its plumbing,
but this far above the water table there's no secret spring

to drink from. Let someone whose face is set
with the rigors of new money take a chain saw to the place

for homelier fires, and fit the bricks to other patios.
I wish one cinder block into fear's repository,

walk it out the beam and let it drop. But the way up
is still the way down, no lighter for having stepped into

someone else's disaster, and just when self-pity
begins to argue that the garden slug, a tube for

excreting and gorging, has the best of life,
a squirrel begins unshingling a pine cone on me.

Over Pond Village, Sladesville, Paine Hollow,
the sky is deepening each night, growing enormous for

Orion and the Wolf Moon. Soon, our roofs under
babushkas of snow, hours when blueness wells from

the footprints of a cat. What are we anyway, but a few
windows mirroring each other, deep in the hills' pockets?

THE RUNE MAN'S WIFE

Sword hafts like Celtic crosses,
a keel propped with stones,
it's not so bad in summer
when he's out walking fields,
hoping to trip on ember boxes
or drop in through a
thousand-year-old crevice
on Vinland-the-Good.

Even his prying after
Thorwald's bones in
clammy cellars,
when they'll let him —
the stares cling to my back,
but they wear thin.

Nights like tonight,
those strange birds
gone from among the flocks,
a North Atlantic vastness
coats the windows with its breath.
While I shudder in bed
he wrestles with it,
brow to brow: a script of
thorns and yoked crow's feet
straggling on his map,
marooned with wine.

I hear a finger
tracing Wonderstrand,
or circling an oval, sandy place.
If a boy rides his bike, just once,

through bearberry, the track remains . . .
Leif's wintering knarr . . .
muttered through my unfinished
walls of sleep.

Tomorrow he'll be fingering
that stone he sees six Skrellings
paddling on, or walking
the shore among brutal evictions,
their soft lives gulped
by alien futures, watching for
prows launched free where surf
has scooped the features off a dune.

Tonight a square sail
pitches in his thoughts,
its tackle snapping.
East of my landfall
he's tuned into the fog.

BACK COUNTRY AUBADE

That moon lit thinly as a demure eyelid
went home. Peepers who whistled tall for her
have quit, and I'm up early after dreaming
an old man who kept no clocks but bushy shadows
edging toward his house.

I keep moments of silence,
edged with coffee filtering, and birds:
the agate calls of crows across a local distance;
unfamiliar notes tossed through the air
like small blue rubber balls;
chips of song fallen out of heaven.

My daughter smuggles a single, muttered word
through sleep.

Space is drawing at my flue:
flame creeps up paper knots,
sure-footed on the backs of old disasters,
and wrists of apple wood
burn to get back to the tree
and bear up handfuls of flowering.

Fragmentary yellow through the pines,
a school bus toils across the dike,
gears catching for the haul up Castle Hill.

A year from this morning, I'll nearly make out
my daughter's voice aboard that chaos,
her lunch box teetering on her head
before the first bell folds her hands.

SCALLOPS

Climbing the jetty
I heard a clicking beyond,
as if the dentures of all
drowned sailors had at last
gained a landfall:

bay scallops,
banked against the stones like
shipwrecked coins, so many
I could have shoveled them into sacks,
their shells varied along
the spectrum of fall ocean:

white of amnesiac fog,
fanned sunrays, the kingfisher's
untrammeled blue.
Others ribbed and slate-colored
as the tide that hoarded them up there
the night before.

They clicked to each other,
the highest bivalves.
They could make me out
through an excess of blue eyes
dotting their gill rakers.

In their element, shells applauding
every move,
they would have leapt away from my hand
a foot at a time,
but up there they would freeze,
or simmer to a stink for
those flying hags, the gulls.

Offshore a loon dipped,
pulling the surface across its back.
As I filled my watch cap
a scallop grabbed my finger
almost playfully.

I was already tasting them shucked,
quick-broiled in butter with
nothing of earth's heaviness
but a sprinkle of parsley.

For them I was glad to risk
passing the no-shellfishing sign,
my hands crossed on the new
belly under my coat
as though I was great with child.

A PHOTO OF MINERS
(USA, 1908)

With trees backing them
instead of the pit's mouth,
they could have been
at a fifth-grade picnic.
But the spitballer won't grow into
his father's jacket, and a ladder
of safety pins climbs the front of
the class clown. Stretch,
who got tall the soonest,
has the air of a chimney sweep,
and here is a little grandfather
in brogans and rag gloves,
his face shoved between two shoulders
his arms are draping,
his eyes flashing the riding lights
of pain. They are a year's
supply, average age, give or take
a year: ten. Don't look for
a bare foot at a devil-may-care
angle on one of the rails,
or a habitable face for a life
you might have led — that
mouth is rigid as a mail slot,
the light on those hands predicts
common graves. Does anything transcend
the walleyed patience of beasts,
the artless smirk on the boy
with the high forehead
who thinks he will croon his way
out of this?

THE INSOMNIA OF BARBERS

They wake up the way anyone would,
except that they pay at union scale
for worrying kids home to mothers about
hollows that could pop open
behind little ears.

These hours all they subscribe to
has expired, including the slack-time issues
whispering acquiescence and black mesh,

and slow as dandruff through an hourglass,
they pay for drinking stories
and mirrors winking all around.

Duennas who wheezed into your privacy,
their loose plates shooting
the air to death,

natty sadnesses with hairs pasted to sunspots,
they are coughing up for every trimming
that's good for another thousand miles.

Tonight they train the pompadour
you had when you studied yourself
in every plate of glass, serious
as a new seminarian. They grease
the wings of your flat-top
till they shine like black leather sleeves.

You they recall as a
foul ball from inning one,
who never took advice
and will thus be parted
on the wrong side forever.

They wish they had lowered your ears
to the deaf level of the floor.

FEAR OF *GRAY'S ANATOMY*

I will not look in it again.
There the heart in section is a gas mask,
its windows gone, its hoses severed.
The spinal cord is a zipper
& the lower digestive tract
has been squeezed from a tube like toothpaste.
All my life I had hoped someday to own
at least myself, only to find I am
Flood's ligaments, the areola of Mamma,
& the zonule of Zinn. Ruffini's endings
end in me, & the band of Gennari lies near
the island of Reil. Though I am a geography
greater than even I surmised, containing as I do
spaces & systems, promontories & at least
one reservoir, pits, tunnels, crescents,
demilunes & a daughter star, how can I celebrate
my incomplete fissures, my hippocampus &
inferior mental processes, my depressions
& internal extremities? I encompass also
ploughshare & gladiolus, iris & wing,
& the bird's nest of my cerebellum,
yet wherever I go I bear the crypts of Lieberkühn,
& among the possible malfunctionaries,
floating ribs & wandering cells, Pott's fracture,
mottles, abductors, lachrymal bones & aberrant ducts.
I will ask my wife to knit a jacket for this book,
& pretend it's a brick doorstop.
I will not open *Gray's Anatomy* again.

CURSE

Enemy, may your house
have too many corners,
in each a spider.

May there be
eight-legged sprinters
without name or number,
and visceral spinners of
topsails and hammocks,
as though your house
was being readied for sea.

If you sweep today, tomorrow
may trampolines and mandalas
hang in the corners, on each
a small war: galleys
rowing through billows and fogs
they turned their insides out for,
engaging whatever falls in,
including yellow buttons of
tansy, planted by superstition
against ants. Though
the ants end like pilots
hung in their chutes above sills
piled with struts and wings,
still, may there be more
ants than spiders. Spray,
and they'll percolate
from one flaw to another,
lugging their dead and unborn
to new inner spaces they've
riddled in walls and beams.

When you sit up in the dark
a hairline will break
and stick to your face
where something has dropped
through your sleep on tenterhooks.
In the morning your shoes
will be attached to lamps,
ceilings to books,
connections only
surrealists can make.

You will ask yourself,
who owns this house where
there are more flaws than
corners, more ants than
spiders? You will
have to get more spiders,
and one day slam the door
on six rooms full of
local fog, or one day
slam the door
and four walls full of
ants will yaw and skew
off their feet.

TO BE HUNG IN A DORMITORY ROOM

You know that end-of-the-semester dream:
you wander corridor to
corridor, a Pentagon-sized
maze as empty as your head,
tiles clicking off
their accusations to your heels
while you look for the door to the exam
you didn't study for because
you signed up in another dream
but woke and missed the lectures,
always in a field you could care less about.
What if you knew that on the night before
the first day of semester
every prof you'll ever have
has gone through the same labyrinth,
and less lucky than you,
finally found the room and cracked the book
so perfectly bound pages lined with
alphabets extinct as great auk tracks
sprang to the air like decks of cards
flexed in his thumb and fingers,
and suddenly a guy in the back row
stood and began to sing,
his Adam's apple working
earnestly to show no threat of campus cops
or blackballs trailing him
from there to sixty-five
would make him sit or quit wearing
the Dutch-boy haircut of the text
to the applaused approval of his peers.

SUPPLIERS DISCOUNT WAREHOUSE

If you were a size 3 or 54,
you might come here to the asphalt's end
where a few cars give off acetylene sunbursts
and the heat crawls up a little into vacancy.
All that remains of a supermarket
is the automatic door and unplugged
produce bin full of rock-bottom markdowns,
no longer seconds, but sixths,
in a debouchment of colors never seen
in nature, but here seven days a week
under one low-overhead roof.
You might come here to be stamped irregular
or to furnish the Terminal Hotel and Lunch
or forage in the air conditioner's ill wind
for the gross contents of anything:
toys the test children walked out on
throwing up their hands, singed sneakers,
the cutlery of torpedoed navies.
Here's a jacket fit for the burial
of a Top Banana, but mangled in the gears
of progress. Here are the mangled
gears themselves, proof that matter
can't be destroyed.
This is a pathos that,
could it declare itself,
would burst into tears and confess everything.

MORNING AFTER

O Rain Black, marry me.
My mirror says superfluous body hair
and blemishes. Whose dress is this
tricked out in chrome to catch
the ballroom lights, whose totaled
pumpkin? The weeds wink gold
flaked off delinquent saurians
and mice, and Conscience, that
swashbuckling cat, keeps jabbing me
with its épée. This prince's
simpering suffusion's over, this floor
is clearly cut with Stumpy,
swarthy Crapulo, and Dummling
pale as his plucked goose. This light's
impossible as your stepmother.
Rise from your pallet underneath
the stairs (you know you're the one
I truly love) and start by
mopping up around my head.

GOOD-BY

21, thumb out in
the breakdown lane,
he's your old man and
you're his almost 20-
year-old lady. The baby's
name is Zeus, the brown dog
is Brown Dog, and
the Revolution is how
you threw home away like
a Girl Scout uniform because
your mother cooked red meat
so you couldn't bliss out.

Between his waffle soles
and your platforms, the orange
backpack from Colorado Sports,
contents: two quarts of Tokay,
an album by Lead Thumb, denims;

his journal, *Hear the music playing
in your mind,* contents:
large *lonliness,* misspelled,
competing on page 1
with a 23-word haiku;
nickle bag, hand-carved bong,
more denim. More and more,
grandmothers are donating
their grins for cryogenics.

The human comedy, except
it's you, incapable of logic
as a setter roaming edges
of an Interstate, licking
its sides sore with a raw tongue,

confused by vans of boredom
drooling lysergic sunsets
on panels like tequila ads.

More and more these nights,
your father dreams himself
into a painting of Rousseau's.
The moon's casaba melon
opens above your mother's
shoulders, the invitation of
her breasts, but the field
is poison ivy
to her waist. She warns him,
Don't come over,
and he doesn't wade in.

BEAR MANIFESTATIONS

1. Bear Under Surveillance

Stoma alert, the maple
reports in first:
he is dreaming of faces
shadowed with thorns

of barbed wire.
In his living room
an angelfish measures
heft and frequency

of his groans.
Blueberries he ate
for dinner
are busily mapping

the intestinal track.
And off Greenland
a pod of right whales
slap their flukes

with laughter.
They have just heard
from percale
his dreamed-up

sexual kinks.
His wife's alligator
purse documents
her hand's travels

through his pants:
the tragic quest
for dollars;
and the last wolf pack

knows time, place, and date
of every impure thought.
At breakfast his watch-
strap sends out

a seismograph
of his pulse.
A grapefruit squirts.
He is marked. Will

nothing let Bear go?

2. Bear Fallen Away

Officially he spilled out through a nave
cracked by translations set to a guitar,
but lack of grace first set him
tripping on a procession of black habits:

at nine he envied Cousin Max
coming back from the rail,
looking like he'd been force-fed
twenty haloes, beads binding
his hands, Christ's masochist.

In high school Bear coveted
the life of the man who thought too much,
condemned to circle the earth
on a tramp steamer. Though lovers
were spitted like shishkababs
in passion-pit motels,
Bear declared himself a hedonist,
moonlighting in his own pines,
wrestling with selected female parts
while limp guys prayed for sainthood.

Pride kept correcting monsignor's Sunday grammar.
The family that prayed together asked for jobs.
One Friday a chicken leg
appeared before him on the way to the abyss.

But he knew he was home free
when he dreamt he was kicking
the bishop, and shouting,
Thus I refute the stone!

3. Bear on God and Man

Theologians quibbled.
Bear imagined a February
which lasted forever,
a stapling of the minor
infractions of every day,
like a breadcrumb trail that wouldn't quit
or arrive at a gingerbread door.

Abstractors were determining the Divine Color,
and whether He or She could build a house
He couldn't lift Herself.

Bear lived in that house.

Which one *was* God, wondered Bear,
the shore of afternoon
a sun has just passed over,
browning the dune's concavities?
(Except where snow lay white
as moonlight falling on itself.)
This scene he observed in silence from the beach.

Or a morning when the wind was easterly
and rammed breath down Bear's windpipe's O,
the grass so mellow

43

when struck its gong flung crows up,
black notes on all that gold?

Or could it matter? Bear wondered
on that vacant shore.

He liked this February.
Bracing on his vertebrae.

4. The Visit of Genius Boy
There visited Bear the following:

2 lines Rimbaud
synopsis of Herman Broch
3 paragraphs Book of Sands
collected letters V. van Gogh
a description:
Great Chestnut of Sunderland, Massachusetts

all in one blue notebook!

After all that
it was looking for a tree
with black leaves.

Wow, Bear yawned.

It was also a theory looking for poems.
Had had the usual visions:

sun once dictated it a complete new name
dream of the woodpecker at the eye
declared greatest poet under thirty
                                by Goneril.

But strangest of all,
what it wanted most was a room by the winter sea.

Well, Bear thought and thought.

Probably buy socks, shave it off.
Shiny suit, move to New Jersey.

and oh, the lies
life forces Bear to tell.
Got mono.
Mother-in-law arriving.
Imminent death of uncle.
Enough false numbers to discombobulate Mother Bell.

After an unhasty lunch it left.

Got to hide, Bear thought.
How about in the Flicker Tree?

5. Bear's Night Letter

Dear Blank. That's how I think of you.
Nameless as your eyes would disclose you
if I got that close.
You may have noticed me, though,
in my window above the street
where I pretend to be switching channels.
I suspect your mother suspects
I have been watching you,
and maybe she is correct to guard
her clothesline, the seven flavors
of your nighties, your pantyhose having a fling
with the breeze. If you think I am humorless
you are wrong. I see the comedy
of those popsicle-colored convertibles
you and your friends jazz around in.
I see your father's pride
when he waters the flowers and you

45

practice handstands or pump your arms
and work over the grunts
of a high-school cheer.
I'm not going to slide out of shadow
with a voice full of peanuts, *Hey, Girlie,*
a crank who stuffs pigeons
into a sack. Oh, no. Secure in my creephood,
it's enough to watch, knowing that one day
perfect teeth enter the pizza
that breaks the cartwheel's back.

6. Bear's Heart with Love Doth Fry, with Fear Doth Freeze

He wanted to be her mystery,
confounding her calculations like
that unlit place under her father's house,
or a basketball thudding once
at the edge of her sleep.

But:

You have the breath of a backwater tarn, she said,
and a pelt no woman would wear,
inside or out.

(This was no good.)

I am the Spirit of Bad Lands,
the places of low sun.
I drink from stone-shored lakes
as they darken with rain,
and free-foot the thin-aired heights
not named for any man
in dead tongues or living,

Bear ragtimed, wondering
should he use incremental repetitions?

Finished? she asked,
and accused him of not understanding Buxtehude.

And when he hid in the shadows
under the maple tree where she walked
her puli, it didn't bare its teeth,
and she didn't drag it home,
its nails etching the sidewalk.
And a good thing, too, Bear thought,
I could rip that mutt like a week-old deli ticket.

And when men zipped on fur suits
and tramped the thaws
in false feet larger than catcher's mitts,

and suddenly, out on the distance,
what looked like a fir tree
stepped from a group and began
crossing the snow field,

Bear stood so long in the midway line
to look at a rubber dummy in a freezer
that ferns grew between his prehensile toes.

FOR THE WAY HOME

Memory's going to try
to make it $2.00 per hour
better than it was, upping
the r.p.m.'s, turning your first car
to a human bomb, intensifying
how rugosa cloyed at roadside
nights you split up puddles
and broke the midges' trance.

Memory puts more hairpin in the turns
where eyepairs glowed
and scrub oak shrieked its warnings
at your sides. Scenes that flew
along your fenders
fell to safety in the trees and grass;
even that bog you chucked the key in
when you went away
is staked for model homes.

Some kid who wanted to be you
unscrewed the stallion off the nose
and when that didn't work
he came back during Deer Week
and fired a supernova through the glass.
Stars that rested on the hood
moved to the roof and trunk,
then slipped off to another state.

At least you're sure you won't end
prowling margins of back roads,
or sweeping public sand through all
the variations of design,
but other than this diamond in the rough,
what was it you told people you'd become?

Remember leaves glued to the roads one fall,
the girl you hoped you'd get
a chance to die for?
Now she's a red-haired woman in
the laundromat. Everywhere
you touched each other is gone,
the details sloughed, a pastel clear
and false as one evening you know
you never saw stretched over town.

THEM

They had their own churches in their own
parts of town, some with domes like onions.
My uncle who got around told me they plastered
money on the pictures, and threw coins
at all the saints. When they died they were buried
standing up. Soon there would be no songbirds
because they ate them with greens
grown around the Virgin and a fruit tree.
My uncle said they did mean things to
the palms of their hands, toughening them
because they didn't know how to take
civil service tests. Their homemade wine
got you snorting like a palomino,
and they locked their daughters in bedrooms
till they clawed the doors like dogs.
He said their doctors were nothing but
thieves in sharkskin, the women were slaves
who scrubbed linoleum on weekends,
and one spring I watched a foreign grampa
paint a picket fence white,
whispering to it on his knees. When my cousin
married one of them with the liquescent
eyes of a bride, my aunt had to leave
the church too early. They threw confetti
on them and drove through town like mad,
honking the horns, with pink and blue
crepe paper on the cars.
After, we ate figs soaked in rum.
In Moramarco's Bakery the cakes were white
and pink, sometimes even blue. All day
Bob worked in the back, his arms powdered from
pushing the dough he chopped to loaves

and slid in the oven on wooden shovels.
On my way home, though my mother
was going to kill me, I ripped off a warm heel
to chew while the winter dusk came down
to four feet off the ground.

WEAVE A CIRCLE ROUND ME THRICE

Before you filled the dark eye
of my uncle
and he taught you to sip oysters
off their shells, confess,
Aunt Eleanore, in your
red-headed days you played the floozy.
More than a whiff of scandal
still attaches to a black dress
wild with flowers unnatural to
Massachusetts. Later the Quaker
Oats pantry and Ma Perkins
seed offers, the breast scar like
a burn that wouldn't heal.
You're the reason I expect
my hand slapped to this day
if I take more than one
piece of candy.

            Aunt Agnes,
for all the chance you had
of marrying, you might as well
have been a tree. Your bathing cap
patterned like tripe, the rubber
slippers stamped with moons and stars,
you sit at Indian Neck and stare
out of the picture, as if down there
a whale was dying
of its stink. You threw *Lolita*
out of my bedroom, tore
the salacious cover off *Lord Jim.*
Paying you back, I picked
your suitcase lock with bent
hairpins, tapping and watering
your private stock. The nephew

closest to a son, I lived with you
ten years, but you don't know me
from my brothers. You walk too near
the traffic, dressed in Peck & Peck,
your mind still on that treadmill
greased by forty years of Standard Oil.

You're in this too, Aunt Delia,
reciting my report cards to
my friends, and reading nieces'
bellies like steamed mail.
It doesn't matter now
who bought the Fords with cash
and never drove them over thirty-five;
which claimed another stole the buttons
off her clothes and took her radio.
One is senile, two are dead.
One thought a sailor stood outside
her window every night, the moon
riding his shoulder like
a cockatoo. One never said "Good-by,"
always "Watch out!" Her blessing
and a prophecy.

        You triple agents,
once I saw you in your denim skirts
and matching red sneakers,
peeking into vacant shops along
Commercial Street.

        That's why,
the night you sneaked up on
my first record hop,
I was in a movie seven miles away.

56

POTSO, MY WINE-DARK UNCLE

I incarcerate you behind
that door with cracked panels,
padlock you at the back of my mind
and throw the key away, until
an evening spills the buttermilk of lethargy
across heights of its going,
and you knock quietly as
the shadow of a whisper you were
at every gathering of the clan.
You are trying to enter, dapper to pointy shoes,
inviting me to give up everything
and follow you, to circle the parking lot
at Mooney's Funeral Home where you've
outlasted temperate sisters like some
dwarf who knows the game by name.
You pencil the winning greyhounds,
even with guts half shot
planning another jaunt to Wonderland.
But you were no original.
Everyone I know had one like you,
and nobody wanted to stumble into your footsteps.
At fifty-five you ran away from home
with a trumpet player's glue-faced wife.
After your ice-cream ride,
for your nacre-button suit and double-breasted
henchman's overcoat, your nephews
raced your landlord up four flights
to a room the smell and color of
an empty mustard jar.

TAR

1

Technically it was liquid asphalt:
MC, RC, 85/100 —
nothing very far removed
from crude, and the floor of
the company barn was stratified
where it dripped off the tank bellies
and pipes of tractor-trailers.

You washed the fumes off skin
same as off trucks:
kerosene sloshed like soap and water,
dabbed around the face,
and at home, soap and water
on the kero, but not before
it could raise red pores along
thighs and cheeks,
and crease you around the eyes.

2

Any time after midnight,
call me helper 64.
I come into the barn with
the Morris brothers, or maybe
Tweet and Lyle, or the Giant,
whose twin I'll later see
in *Introductory Genetics*.

To check the List we have to pass
Magliese, the night dispatcher,
sleeping like a company cat
but waking at a step,
and short on greetings.

58

Tonight I go with driver 8
somewhere between the Androscoggin River
and the Hudson, praying it won't be
a penetration job on an expressway
where July piles 96 on
500 degrees of asphalt.
Better a prelunch mix-and-place
up country, then the luxury
of sleep on overtime among New Hampshire daisies.
Better yet, a rainout and layover.

3

But who is driver 8?
3 is Godfrey Farrington, lordly
drunken as his name, who'll look
by 6 A.M. for lit cafés
to square himself away in.

The Giant is 7, and 12
is someone with a car
and girl friend sunk in Chelsea Creek,
and 70 hours on the clock.
Nodding at the wheel, he'll
see things in the road
and plead, *Keep talking to me, kid.*

4 is an acrophobe, eyes
shut on bridges; 15 they call
The Naphtha King: one spark
and we're the hottest thing in town.

For a cure, TB patients
ran the rear motor

when Jack Hayward broke in.
Helpers get crazy, kid. The heat.
With drivers it's the kidneys,
all these pot holes on bum springs.
Save your dough, and quit.

4

When I who escaped try to imagine
a heaven for those true fly-by-nights
who sprayed earth
with the nether world's hot fossils,
I see a place where logbook entries
satisfy the I.C.C. and gauges work
so nobody runs kero through the tank
to stretch the job and pacify a slide rule.
There a holiday is more than a gap
down the middle of a road
where two black strips don't overlap.
Jackie Howard tightens his tank cap right,
saving his skin this time,
and the Jack-O-Lantern Grill is open
beyond closing, its booths full of girls
to talk to and take home.
Punched in the gut, Lowell Frenchie
never goes down, and whatever
flames upon the night
isn't Monsanto Chemical or Esso.

PETER

Kneeling into the life
of a marsh, looking beyond yourself
for navies who long after us
will emerge and reorganize
under the sun,
how many times have you split
muddy knees and come home
with a sore throat that felt
like a smile you swallowed?
Fall, and you came with a cocoon;
all winter we moved around it:
a wad of exhausted gum
stuck on a branch in a jar
out of the sun.
Ah, Mr. Science, Dr. Dirt,
why do you care
what the moon weighs?
Too soon the man with the answers
will step from unlit recesses, the beard
of your confusion will begin.
Then you will be more
than the son we have always wanted.
But this afternoon, while the pavement
swam with mirages, your jar
began to crawl with live brown rice.
And now there are mantises
seeding the air, and twilight in which
you claim possums will stir
and creep into city yards.

THE FIELD OF INHERITANCE

(for Anne)

1

In your drawings
my face is one-celled,
each eye floating like a centrosome.
Hairs of my beard
have reverted to cilia,
and I think how you came to us
from beyond the press of water and earth.

2

When I hear you saying
you don't want to die and go
where there are no people,
I wish I could jack death's jaws
like it was something
that stands up nightly in
the corners of your room.
I wish I could skin it for you
as you've seen me
take the hide off a tautog.
But whatever we call it,
if we litanize it, whining,
O Keeper of Last Darkness,
or give it names so rotten
our breaths back up and we gag,
death won't come out in the open
and fight us fair.

3

When my friend nearly drowned
off Hatteras,
he saw our images rise
in a flurry of bubbles
like rainbowed homunculi.
He saw you and me stare like sheep
as we flew in the surf on our sides,
taking it easy because
there was nothing for us,
only that listening toward
our hearts until each
flicker of pain deserted our eyes.
Blackballed to breath on a wave,
he wakes to his mind
frisking itself for something,
each night he knows how the dead
and the living return to each other.

4

But merely because of death
do not become one of those
for whom the earth is a boulder
cast into the dark
and the spirit like a fish
thick as a pasture stone
on the ocean's floor, its lips
working like a doubled inner tube,
its gills and fins trying horribly
to be wings.

A queen who wore your name
gave it to these snowcups
flowering out of your great-grandfather's
carrots gone to seed,
running wild with his
asparagus that are frail as
the limbs of daddy-long-legs.
In this field, what's delicate
survives, spilling uphill toward
your uncle's place beyond those butterflies
sparring or tying love knots in the air.

5

Don't be too sure
when the Queen Anne's lace
leans to you and you tell it,
"Go away, you're not my daughter."

And on the day
life tempts you to think
it consists of the crow
we saw on route 6 once,
knee deep in fox with the sun
a veneer of butter
streaking across hot steel a feather away,
remember the sprig of parsley
we shared together here,
the frill of vitamin A
that grew all winter
out of garden snow.

NEEDSONG

Sweetmeat, what we need is a tune
scored in bedrock, something
that leaks out of burrows in the grass
& keeps alive one twitch
someplace. We'll both be under
sometime anyway, maybe of something
unmentionable, like intracardial
traduction, with two rich surgeons
still in their twenties
standing over us mumbling
"reverse breach contractor," &
"post-affection decimation ratio."
We've already believed in
so many things that are wrong,
why not one more interlude
for the living, something to sing
when the odor of pears from a bag
sticks us back in the first grade
far from torts & the tarot,
where the sky can look in windows
& see the doorway & our mothers
unknotting our fists from theirs
& nudging us over the oiled floors
toward Miss Stone. O Dark Lady,
remember: the twenty-six letters
you couldn't read & those sullen
janitors downstairs shoveling
into their hives? The baby's
the age my sister was when
the half-moons were drawn
in death's kohl under her eyes
& the blue bows in her hair
couldn't hide her bones being readied

for their flight. This is
a song about ampersands. I know
you've got my troubles & I've
got yours: we need a tune that'll
iron out the whole convolvulus
& settle scores of worry on our
foreheads, something a couple of kids
can whistle on the paths among the trees.

THE KIDS

They are the reasons you say
everything three times, the ritual
for getting nothing done
while the holes in your socks
move from arch to heel,
charting the growth of
your son's feet as they break
out of his shoes like tubers.

One night your daughter screams
she's going crazy here
and you know it's not just
the moon, but someone she's found
who has all your bad habits.

So they inherit you layer by layer,
a roll of bills peeled off
till you are revealed as Dagwood
at the center, throwing
your hands in the air
and yelling What good?

This is called "learning the pain
of tenderness," or is it
"the tenderness of pain"?
You are the only orchard
where your son's bruises
ripen to rare fruits.
That dream was yours alone
where your daughter became a doll
swinging from your arm.

And these are the only answers
to the riddle: What costs you everything?

ANSWERING A QUESTIONNAIRE, "ON LIVING WITH AN ARTIST," SENT TO MY WIFE

Our marital status is Married,
and we are Living Together, too,
not the first time for such an arrangement.
Strangely, these kids live with us,
hence this litter, the room of a crank
who collects and tears up the news,
these playpen and knapsack detours,
brine shrimp swimming in glasses
we drink out of to our peril,
and a pissy pants Electra dragging me off this page.
(Each of her steps is a nail hammered home, another
gray hair, clothes flung to her suitcase's maw
and an open door.)

Oh Yes, we'd do it again. I would, in spite
I'm so happy sometimes it's scary.
I worry my heart will unstring
and sail off like a kite. I think
only heavy payments are keeping me on the ground.
Love, friendship, stability, security,
encouragement, nerves of steel
and a strong mailbox, not always in that order.

We make the time, though unlike when love
was illegal entry and we forged our way
past *deja vus* of lobbies,
the landlady gets her knowing twitch
and calls my love to coffee,
or boneless, black-and-white men
with briefcases and Bibles (humorless angels
or F.B.I.?) appear at the front door.

Students take my picture, but aside
from Church, State, and Big Business, I haven't been
the target of predators, and Yes,
I'm interested in daily life,
but not, I would guess, overly. Sometimes
I fall so deep between words
she has to call me back, although since
she handles the finances I'm as often
on the sidewalk without a dime to call home.
We talk them out, and you've just started one:
she says we argue least about the consistency
of peanut butter, I say it's over
the state of veterinary medicine.

It's all subject to circumstance, some
find it hard not to marry. But generally
your questionnaire implies that artists are
abnormal. Let me say in closing
I lied: I didn't show this to her.
Contortions of Yes and No are for 3 A.M.
We both sleep soundly.

IN ENVY OF INSTINCT

Earth, air, or water,
which are we natural to?
Running the country
the only way I know how,
I put one foot
before another, where
earlier a deer clicked off
the distance like a caliper.

My heart beats red
as the pouch
of a horny frigate bird.
My lungs are sponges
working for more air.
When I stop,
a metaphor for nonchalance
comes paddling up the creek.

Is it speech and its procrastinations
that separate us
from these lower orders?
Or that backlash of knots
and loops, the ultimate
nervous system? Any wave skimmer
belting along the coast
could go without reason
to Venezuela tomorrow.

Off Jeremy Point the bluefish
hang straight out in midair;
seeing them flexed
over fleeing bait,
my heart stands up
and walks into my throat.

Surely this body's more than just
support for a tangle of untied punch lines,
out-takes from The Impossible,
and mash notes from the dead?
Why can't I have a woman
with breasts like the mourning doves?

And goddam it I'd like
the energy ants save the world with.
To store it drib by drab in undermines
and riddles of wood, no jot too small
from smears and flakes,
from lips of children asleep.
A decimal at a time, to carry off
whole silos, nudging the origin
of species my way.

DIAGNOSIS

Between flesh and the spirit,
who's not torn?
A hairless curate
trails around in me
on rubber soles:
his homilies are fluent
as birch rods.
He trims my wicks.
A notebook in his skirts
lists my offenses
by the ounce.
He calls the shots
all right (let's call him
A).

Though there's B, too,
who wants and will not quit.
He's the unstrung Harp
who framed me for
pratfalls. Just hear him,
day and night:
Kick out the skids!
ditched on his back
in weeds beside the road.
Oh, he's the nightsweat's
father, I know that,
Will-o'-the-Wisp
dry in the throat,
who nails his warning
flare to my big toe.

Then when his deathbed
pillow's plumped, he's randy
for the candles and the oil.
But A produces chalk,
and, on the clearing
blackboard of B's skull,
describes delicious tits.

B knocks the blocks out then,
goes with his goad
and dams the tilted bucket.
Think of the chicken
and the egg, or
partners in a dance hall
marathon, marrying
each other
through the night.
Think of diastole
and systole,
stick in a barrel
beating good times out.

THE OLD CLOTHES

Often I visit them where they slump
in the closet, hangers protruding
like beggars' shoulder blades.
Splotched as if they'd endured
barrages of fruit, as if the body,
short-circuiting, let go its fluids
and salts, a blowout frazzling cuffs
and throwing off buttons
like a millionaire flinging coins
in his old neighborhood,
I should cram them in a poor box
in some parking lot far from home,
except they'd be back that night,
cowering or stiff as the line-up,
pockets bagged for larceny
or deflated by keyholes, derailed
and toothless zippers, knees
weak as unanswered prayers.
I should pay some crone
to slash up the lot
and hook me a rug for my old age,
something to keep on my lap
and pick up a clue from —
some thread of evidence
that proves I was going straight.

PITT POETRY SERIES

Paul Zimmer, General Editor

Dannie Abse, *Collected Poems*

Adonis, *The Blood of Adonis*

Jack Anderson, *The Invention of New Jersey*

Jack Anderson, *Toward the Liberation of the Left Hand*

Jon Anderson, *Death & Friends*

Jon Anderson, *In Sepia*

Jon Anderson, *Looking for Jonathan*

John Balaban, *After Our War*

Gerald W. Barrax, *Another Kind of Rain*

Leo Connellan, *First Selected Poems*

Michael Culross, *The Lost Heroes*

Fazıl Hüsnü Dağlarca, *Selected Poems*

James Den Boer, *Learning the Way*

James Den Boer, *Trying to Come Apart*

Norman Dubie, *Alehouse Sonnets*

Norman Dubie, *In the Dead of the Night*

Odysseus Elytis, *The Axion Esti*

John Engels, *Blood Mountain*

John Engels, *The Homer Mitchell Place*

John Engels, *Signals from the Safety Coffin*

Abbie Huston Evans, *Collected Poems*

Brendan Galvin, *The Minutes No One Owns*

Brendan Galvin, *No Time for Good Reasons*

Gary Gildner, *Digging for Indians*

Gary Gildner, *First Practice*

Gary Gildner, *Nails*

Mark Halperin, *Backroads*

Michael S. Harper, *Dear John, Dear Coltrane*

Michael S. Harper, *Song: I Want a Witness*

Samuel Hazo, *Blood Rights*

Samuel Hazo, *Once for the Last Bandit: New and Previous Poems*

Samuel Hazo, *Quartered*

Gwen Head, *Special Effects*

Milne Holton and Graham W. Reid, eds., *Reading the Ashes: An Anthology of the Poetry of Modern Macedonia*

Shirley Kaufman, *The Floor Keeps Turning*

Shirley Kaufman, *Gold Country*

Abba Kovner, *A Canopy in the Desert: Selected Poems*

Paul-Marie Lapointe, *The Terror of the Snows: Selected Poems*

Larry Levis, *Wrecking Crew*

*T*HIS first edition of

THE MINUTES NO ONE OWNS

consists of fifteen hundred copies

in paper cover, five hundred copies

hardbound in boards,

and fifty specially bound copies

numbered and signed by the author.